PULVER
MAAR

Pulver Maar
Poems 2014-2018

Zachary Schomburg

Black Ocean
Boston · Detroit · Chicago

To reprint, reproduce, or transmit electronically, or by recording all or part of this manuscript, beyond brief reviews or educational purposes, please send a written request to the publisher at:

Black Ocean
P.O. Box 52030
Boston, MA 02205
blackocean.org

Cover Design by Dennis Schmickle | dennisschmickle.com
Book Design by Nikkita Cohoon | nikkita.co

ISBN 978-1-939568-27-4

Library of Congress Cataloging-in-Publication Data

Names: Schomburg, Zachary, 1977- author.
Title: Pulver Maar : poems 2014-2018 / by Zachary Schomburg.
Description: Boston : Black Ocean, [2019] | Includes bibliographical
    references and index.
Identifiers: LCCN 2018061271 | ISBN 9781939568274 (paperback : alk. paper)
Subjects: LCSH: American poetry--21st century.
Classification: LCC PS3619.C4536 A6 2019 | DDC 811/.6--dc23
LC record available at https://lccn.loc.gov/2018061271

FIRST EDITION

CONTENTS

INSIDE WE MAKE CHILDREN SANDWICHES

NOW IS A GOOD TIME

AVIARY AREA

OARS

HAIRCUTS

THE FUTURE / THE BABY

INSIDE WE MAKE
CHILDREN SANDWICHES

PULVER MAAR

There once was a maar named Pulver Maar. Pulver Maar loved being a maar. It loved its rim and its footpath, and it loved its phreatomagmatic eruptions and its bathing place. But what it loved most of all was its dove. Like all doves, its dove was a dove of love. The dove dove down deep. It dove down deep into the maar's love. Where it is warm. And where it is made.

THE CLOUD

The cloud fell in love with the woman, and the woman fell in love with the cloud. The cloud sat on the woman's head like a big white hairdo. The cloud was the biggest and whitest hairdo anyone had ever seen. Together, they shined bright, an afternoon of true magic. Some clouds spent their moment casting shadows, but not my cloud, said the woman years later, shivering now, uncontrollably now, in a snow drift, on the white plains.

PEACH WHO THINKS

There once was a girl named Peach who loved to think. She stayed in her room all day thinking about everything outside of the room—a skein of black geese, the way a telephone feels in the hand, life on the moon. Peach's family would linger at the dinner table each night to talk, but she would always excuse herself early, to go off thinking. There are not enough minutes in a life, she thought, and then she thought about that too, about all the minutes she had left. Time surrounded her, mockingly, like a field in a field.

SHU FANG AND
THE BOTFLY

One morning, Shu Fang fell in love with the tiny
botfly growing and throbbing and turning red
inside the crown of her head. She loved that tiny
botfly with all of her body, and it was that love that
made her botfly grow. It was the first thing Shu
Fang ever loved that was all her own, that no one
else loved too. All day she would touch it under
her hat, and all night, while her mother and father
slept, Shu Fang would listen to its fluttering echo
in her ears. Before long, the tiny botfly wasn't tiny
anymore, and it shook and bit and broke its way
out of Shu Fang's head. Shu Fang was so happy to
hold it in her hands, to look in its eyes and love
it, but the looking and loving never happened.
The botfly just flew around the room breaking
everything, and when it looked back into her eyes,
over the broken dishes, over the bloody bodies
of Shu Fang's mother and father, it looked as if
it wanted to break her too. It looked more like a
thing, like a cold and unholdable buzzing thing,
than the thing Shu Fang loved. Shu Fang knew
how impossible it would be from then on for her
to love any and all of the things that live on the
outside of her bleeding and gaping head. Now I'll
only love my blood, she thought. And she thought,
now I'll only love my gape.

BOB THE BUOY

There once was a buoy named Bob the Buoy who bobbed in center of the sea. Bob's job was to tell the boats where the sea was deepest. He bobbed and bobbed, all night, all alone, waiting for a boat, but no boat ever came. The lonely nights lasted days and days. Until one night, a boy swam right up to Bob. "Are you a boat?" asked Bob. "No, I'm a boy," said the boy, exhausted. The boy started climbing up so he could rest on the top of Bob. That made Bob feel happy. "Why are you here?" asked Bob. "Our boat shipwrecked, and I've been stranded alone in the sea," answered the boy. "Just like me," said Bob. "Not anymore," said the boy. Bob made the boy very happy too. "Why did your boat shipwreck?" asked Bob. "We didn't know how deep the sea was," answered the boy. Then the boy fell asleep on top of Bob. Bob fell asleep too. Then a boat came and waked Bob the Buoy and the boy up. "It's a boat!" they both exclaimed in unison. The captain of the boat thanked Bob the Buoy for saving the boy, then they left Bob alone, forever, bobbing in the sea, waiting for another boat. Bob bobbed and bobbed, waiting and waiting for another boat to tell it how deep the sea was where he bobbed. Bob missed the boy very much. But he was the happiest buoy any buoy had ever been.

THE DUST AND THE CRUST

There once was a little piece of dust that was scared of everything. It was scared of being eaten by insects, and it was scared of the light, and in those moments of being scared, the piece of dust felt most alone. It spent all day being scared of the air, tumbling and floating around in it, when it finally settled upon the toaster. Irene, the very old owner of the house, cleaned on Tuesdays, and the little piece of dust knew it. It was, needless to say, very scared. Irene was very mean, and she liked to keep her old house clean. But on this particular Tuesday, Irene was far too hungry to clean. So, she just put bread in the toaster. The little piece of dust was, of course, scared it would get too hot, but just before it got too hot, up popped toast. Like everything else in the world, even the toast scared the little piece of dust, how it popped up with such a force. The toast was made of gluten, and Irene wasn't supposed to have gluten, so before she could clean off the toaster, she died. Her mouth opened wide as she died, and a little piece of crust fell from her lips, and fell gently onto the toaster, right next to the little piece of dust. The little piece of crust and the little piece of dust became best friends, and for the rest of its life, the little piece of dust was never scared of anything ever again.

THE SICK LITTLE BOY FROM WELLINGTON

The sick little boy from Wellington sneaked out from his family's bedroom flat late one night while his parents slept soundly and healthily. He was sick of being sick, and sick of being worried about and sick of being doted over. *Would you like another spot of chamomile? Is your forehead too hot?* No more, thought the sick little boy from Wellington, and so he set out this night to trudge in his wellies in the snow. It is time I set out to make my own self well, he thought. But within a few minutes of his trudging, he slipped on a patch of ice, went arse over tit, and lost his inhaler in the snow. On his back, just around the corner from his slumbering parents, the stars shone warm and bright like hot coals in a hot furnace, and then out came his very last hot breath, but from the very tip of his tiny willy.

THE FAMILY OF TINY CATS

Gertie walked to her dead grandmother's house only to find her grandmother dead on the floor. She cried, then she sent out a few letters, and then she arranged a funeral, and everyone her grandmother ever loved and everyone who ever loved her back attended it, and they all looked nice in their dresses and their suits, and they all laughed and told stories about Gertie's grandmother, and then Gertie went back home to make some hot soup, to make some very, very special hot soup.

WANDA ONE ARM

Wanda One Arm was climbing a mountain when she found an arm balancing on the tip of the mountain's peak. The arm was all alone. It had no body to be on. Wanda worried, and Wanda wondered about who the arm belonged to. Is this your arm you're missing? Wanda asked the mountain goat, but clearly this was no mountain goat arm. Is this your arm you're missing? Wanda asked the buzzard, but this arm had no feathers. So, Wanda carried home the arm tucked in the pits of her own one arm. Once home, she asked her mom. Does this arm belong to Grandpa? But her grandpa was dead and buried with both arms intact. Wanda took out an ad in the newspaper. Whose Arm? read the ad above a photograph Wanda took of the arm. She wrote a song about it on the piano, and sang the song out of her windows every day. No one responded. No one claimed the arm as their own. It was the arm of the mountain, determined Wanda. And so it was the arm of the mountain. The next day Wanda returned it to the tip of the mountain, and balanced it there, just like she found it.

LUIS AND THE BOX KITE

Luis's father died, so Luis built a box kite to keep himself company. When Luis flew the box kite, he lost his grip on the string. He was very upset at himself, for he had no more wood, and no more string, to build another box kite. The box kite just drifted over the mountains, its string either waving goodbye or reaching blindly for a hand. I love you, Luis said.

NOW IS A GOOD TIME

NOW IS A GOOD TIME

It takes forever for the bandages
to come off then they do.
She's younger than anyone
could've seen. Try spending
20 minutes seeing the young.
See how young someone
you've never met can get.
What are the distances
between beauties? Me,
I want my lumps
to be little clouds
over the garden.

THE DISTANCE OF LOVED ONES

What a wonderful park
and wonderful air
just like the air
I remember. I'm me
thinking all my thoughts
like a man showing
my I.D. walking backward
between the girls
on horses going in circles.
Can you really be anywhere?
I would kiss the boy
version of myself if my father
who is my age wasn't
staring at us. This is a
wonderful time for you,
boy me. Enjoy the summer
is all I've ever really wanted
to tell you.

SOMETHING'S IN THE AIR

There are 8,900,
000 germs in one
cubic foot of air.
You leave the window
open wide for
the devil, so the devil
fills the room with
its special fatness.
Everything's in order.
Your hearts are normal.
Your hearts are beaten
normal with boredom.
I take a deep breath
and push you through
the window. All the way
down you whisper
I will make you
a potato pancake.

BETTER BUSINESS BUREAU

The typewriter is typing
I'm going to kill you.
There's a boy on the lawn
working on the same
blue popsicle. I'd like
to be chased to a lip
of something, anything,
a ship's plank, or a cliff,
or the swimming pool
by my self. I mean
I want to be chased
by my own body, or
by my self in my own
car. You'd be shocked
at how long I can
wait in a long line
when I'm prepared to file
the complaint of my life.

THE POTOMAC CLUB!

You really have to
put more coins in
the coin slot to know
the future. The future
is we've always lived
in Saint Louis. Right
in the center. In
the arch, even.
In a cute apartment
at the top of the arch.
The only apartment.
It's a secret, like
everything else in Saint
Louis, you have to
have a secret password.
What's the secret
password, you ask?
The secret password is
the potomac club!

LIFE DURING THE FUTURE

Who fingered the clicker
wasn't exactly Ms.
Culture 2020, wasn't
wearing a fur coat
for a camera, didn't
come from witches.
The paintings ain't
Mings, and the Louis
XIV candelabras are
phonies, but they'll
be stolen by a certain
kind of people. Just
not us, not you and me.
We're people, sure,
but what kind of people?
Horses. More specifically,
race horses named
Tiny Tutu.

MORE ABOUT GRAVITY

I remember this one
planet, how it had
these two people
kissing on the lip
of a big volcano.
I used to watch them
every night, in the
fuzzy lens of my
telescope. Each time
they'd get too excited
and tip in. Come
home, I said alone
in my room to no one
and no one ever did.

I'LL GET ON A LLAMA

I'll get on a llama
just to see where it
takes me. (Throwing
my foot now over
its spine). Oh no,
just as I suspected.

SELLING TRINKETS AT THE FUNERAL

All The Mangler ever
wanted was a good
crowd, and that's what
he got. His father came,
for example, and his
daughter too, and his
daughter's husband,
and that man's son.
Everyone brought their
own brand of sadness.
The funeral was so popular
the sadness overwhelmed.
It was so sad the horse
was shaped like an M.
Everyone was too sad
to eat so they
started starving.
People were running
over children's legs.
The only thing that
can save us now
no one thought to say
is that thing that
would never save itself.

THE LAST LEG OF PROVIDENCE

You left yr bar of soap
in my shower.
My neighbor is watching
television. "Go! Go!"
Things get small then disappear.

RIGHT MAN FOR THE JOB

I saw a man coming
in the distance but
I couldn't make out
who it was. He was
coming on a horse.
It'll all be over in
just a few short hours,
I said to my wife.
And it sure was.
Afterwards, we spent
our entire lives crying.
But the good thing
about crying is you
don't really have to
pick a subject.

THE SUNRISE LASTS FOREVER

You're doing a great
job lifting five people
above your own head,
The Mangler, Jr.
But you're just making
everyone miss your
father. He was so
unnaturally strong.
I remember once when
you were a baby, how
he lifted five people
while lifting you too.
He was so kind too.
And beautiful. He
had such beautiful
hair and skin, and
when he spoke,
his tongue floated
above the heads of
everyone in the room
licking the evil away
and freeing them
from the evil that
held them hostage
in their own hearts.
I wish you luck,
young man.

SANJOO HUH

You called me on
your cell phone
to tell me you were
on a llama riding
through the mountains
in search of a girl
who had been kidnapped
last week. My cell
phone is breaking up,
you said. Sanjoo,
I am sure
it is my cell phone
that is causing
the problem, I said.
Anyway, it doesn't matter
whose cell phone
is at fault. I hear
it's lovely in Peru.
Sanjoo, I hear
it is lovely in Peru.
In Peru! It's lovely!

A NOVEL ABOUT A HOUSE

I'm writing a novel
about a house
that has a dream
of being a stand-up
comedian. It takes
a bus to L.A. but
everyone gets upset.
The house takes up
a whole row of seats.
No one believes that
the house will make it.
There's nothing funny
about it. It's a ranch.

A NOVEL ABOUT A COW

I'm writing a novel
about a cow
that thinks it's
the Queen of Bavaria.
It wears a red cape.
One day, a girl milks it
in a way it does not
like to be milked.
That's how it starts.

THE ASTRONAUTS

We were sitting on
the front porch after
a long day of yard
work. The hydrangea
is beautiful, I said.
Fuck the hydrangea,
you said. You were
tired. I could tell.
I knew how you felt
about the hydrangea,
and I shouldn't have
brought it up. Anyway,
it was important now
to change the subject.
Your mother is on a
train to Pittsburgh
right now. Isn't it so
romantic, taking the train
these days, I said.
Fuck the train, you said.
After I thought about it
for a while, I knew you
were right. It was stupid
for your mother to take
the train, let alone to Pittsburgh.
The moon was so full.

It looked like we could
just reach up and touch it.
Have you ever wondered
what it'd be like, I said,
to just walk around
in a new world, to be
the first person to be
in a world. When I
looked over, you were
asleep. Your breathing
had already started
to change, like you weren't
quite getting enough air.
Like I said, it had
been a very long day.

THE NEIGHBORHOOD IS CHANGING

Yesterday, my husband told
me he felt like a musk ox.
I didn't know what to say.
Are you just going to sit
there, he said. I don't know
what to say, I said. That's just
like you, he said. Do you
feel like a musk ox right now,
I said, trying. Would you
ask a musk ox if he felt
like a musk ox right now,
he said. He makes a good
point. It's rare to know
a musk ox as smart as my
husband. I looked out
of the living room window
and felt so defeated.
Everything was changing.
I didn't know who anybody
was anymore. It was hard
to know who even I was.
It's clear we're in a real rut,
I said. I've been reading
about this very thing,
he said.

IT IS A LOW LIFE

Something starts happening.
Then something is happening.
Then something happens.
And then nothing happens.
And then something new happens.
Then you jump off a tall building
and die on the sidewalk
in front of a group of school
children on a class field trip
to the natural history museum.
There is a big statue of
a mammoth out front.
It has long bronze tusks.
Some of the school children
touch the bronze tusks.
Some of them even hang
from the tusks, even though
they were told not to.
Some play in the blood.

THE SNOWY PLOVER
OF RENO

Something evil happened
on the great shores
of Washoe. I felt death
would come from beneath
the water. I called upon God,
only to hear his very last
word. I startled him
into a coughing fit.
The timing was just
awful. Help, he said.
Great, I thought, God's dead.
Just then, a snowy plover
swooped down and bit
my eyeball. Now I had
only one good eye.
Do you know how hard
it is to find a good job
these days? A whole half
of the world is lost
to me now. I walk now
only in circles to know
what in my life is coming.

I AM A WHITE HORSE

I am a white horse wandering
an empty planet. Everything on
this planet is beautiful, untouched
and clean. And I am so beautiful
too, and strong. Sometimes,
I spend a whole week being
a white horse. But in real life,
everything is going to hell.
I haven't taken the trash out
for weeks. The stench is getting
harder to ignore. My neighbor,
Betty, was so concerned that
she came over the other day.
She found me in the kitchen
with my shirt off. I whinnied
at her. "Bonnie," she said,
"you're not a horse." "Right,"
I said, "I'm not just any horse.
I am the only horse." "No,
you're no horse at all," she said,
"just look at you." I looked down
at my body, but all I could see
was the white white horse of
my body. "Your life is falling apart,"
she said, holding her nose.
"And your house is disgusting."

I finally conceded. It had quickly
become too much to bear. Then
Betty took a big breath and said,
"Bonnie, you're disgusting too."
I asked her to leave. I only
wanted to be a white horse,
alone, wandering in the beautiful
world. "It's true," she said
from outside the house now
through the open kitchen window
the open field behind her, her head
tilted to the side to show off
her empathy. "Even your nipples,"
she cried. "They're like little socks
of hamburger."

SOLAR ECLIPSE OVER MT. KINANGOP

I carried our sick baby
in a fishbowl on a train
through the mountains
toward the doctor.
Many years later,
the nun next to me
on the plane prayed
I wouldn't die and
when I didn't die
I had to eat her.

A NOVEL ABOUT A PANCAKE

I'm writing a novel
about a pancake
that a member of the pancake
club, held each Sunday
at Little Piggy's
between 34th and 35th
on Maple, took home
with her because she
couldn't finish it.
It killed her cat
the next day, minutes
after she tried to feed it
the pancake. Anyway,
it'll never work.
You just don't eat pancakes
like that. You eat
them in stacks.

A NOVEL ABOUT A SECRET LAKE

I'm writing a novel
about a secret lake
that everyone knows about
except for one person,
a bitter older man
named David who
collects swords.
Everyone gives their word
they won't tell David
about the secret lake.
Things go well like that
for a few years. A few
near accidental revelations
in casual conversations
but no major slip ups.
Then David dies in
a suspicious (you guessed it)
sword accident. Everyone
walks around shaking
their heads, visibly upset,
but not about David.
The lake, one of them says
at the end, it'll never
be the same.

THE DISTANCE OF LOVED ONES

When I was a baby I was
kidnapped from my bassinet.
My mother was soaking
in the bathtub. She couldn't
hear the intruder walk
down the hallway
and open my bedroom
door because the hot water
from the faucet was
splashing into the tub.
The hot water turned
the cold water back
into hot water. The suds
were so high around her.
She rubbed the suds
on her legs which were
in the air. She started at her
ankles and then she moved
the suds up over her knees
and then she moved her hands
down into the hot water
where the suds stayed on
the surface and where her
hands kept going down
beneath the surface

down between her legs
and they stayed there.
Her knees fell away
to the sides of the tub
and her head fell
all the way back.
Then out came a
little baby scream.

HIGH JOHN
THE CONQUERER

I like to tell a story about
High John the Conquerer
that focuses overwhelmingly
on his rage, how it comes
down upon his kingdom
suddenly, like a storm,
and how he demands gifts—
falcons in cages, particularly,
to quell it. Upon hearing
this, you excuse yourself.
You forgot something in
your car. Then from the car
window, you yell you forgot
to turn off your stove.
You drive away in all
directions at once.
It's remarkable how you
do it, how you split
yourself into four
fields, four colorful planes
of existence to move
forever and always in.
I have proof now,
I think, of the roundness
of a world. A world
where wherever you go
you go away.

FALCON

A falcon at its saddest
is bending an arc.
The sky holds a cloud
in it like a blue heart.
We walk into a room
and we turn on a lamp.
The rooms we fell
in love in are still
there, by rule,
beaming a wet
beam over the city.
I've lost my top.
I am topless
in the city, boatless
in a great blackness,
a wide black sea,
lit from above
by a sun spinning
away in the distance,
a heat meant for
someone else.
You may have this
exploding light—
my only true light.

ACCIDENT WAITING TO HAPPEN

It had been waiting there
on the corner all day
to happen in the smothered
heat of the shade.
A woman rode by on
a bicycle with her baby
covered in the basket,
when she noticed.
"What are you waiting
for?" she said. "To happen,"
said the accident, politely.
"It's too hot for that,"
she said. "But what
about the baby?" said
the accident. "Oh no!"
said the woman, "What baby!?"

A MOUNTAIN'S JOB IS
TO JUT

It's true, I did get fired
from the globe factory.
I put a beach in N.D.
and us on it but then
I put us in the waves
in a bed on the waviness.
It's best to just put things
where you think you
want them. When I think
of mountains I think
of beer, and how clean
everything can be.
When I think of buoys
I think of the darkness.
But also I think of seals.
An island is the wrong
symbol for loneliness.
I never wanted two cats.
Now I have nothing
in cats.

CONGRATS ON YOUR NEW JOB

Your new job is to sit
behind a desk and click
the metal clicker every
time a new person walks
in. In your excitement,
you click the clicker
on accident. But it's ok,
you think. You just tell
yourself to not click
the clicker when the next
person walks in. But
no one else walks in.
Hours go by. You think
maybe someone is about
to come in, so you click,
forgetting that you weren't
supposed to click for
the next person. Now
you're two clicks ahead.
It's the end of the day.
You go home, but you
never go back. It's just
not the job for you.
You spend the rest of
your life like that,

two clicks ahead,
like a fly pinned
to the meridian.

THE COW

I befriended the cow
on my trip to the farm.
The two of us were
inseparable. I knew
how to make it moo.
But that was so many
years ago. Whose farm
even was that? I don't
really remember. There's
whole swaths of my life
of which I can't even
recall the tiniest things.
One thing I think I do
remember is how wise
the cow was. It said things
like never be afraid
and never give up.
Hold on to hope
and learn from your
mistakes. Don't
be so in love all
the time. It gets in
the way. Stop loving.
Stop wanting to be loved.
Stop loving yourself
so much. Stop letting
love into your life.
Stop eating so much
dairy.

FALLING FOR THE WILY ONE

That wily Jamunapari had a beard
I couldn't stop stroking.
We spoke without speaking
for what seemed like
an hour, and then it
bleated a bleat of real love,
or something that sounded
disproportionately like love.
Suddenly, I remembered
my past life, or maybe
it was a future life.
I was on a bumpy train
to only God knows where.
My conical teats shook
almost imperceptibly.
That's when the big one
came. It came in six
to ten silent and sorrowful
pulses. When I opened
my eyes, I was looking
at a patch of amaranth
on a new cliff, over-
looking a different
cliff in the distance.
I had yet to know
that goat, a world
overfilled with bridges.

OFF WE GO AMOUNTING
TO SOMETHING

The doctor's job was
to hold things.
She held a baby
then she held a cat.
She held some trophies
for being a doctor.
She showed me her
trophies and told me
about each one.
This one's for holding hearts
she said. This one's
for just looking at blood
she said. The blood
trophy was a little smaller
than the heart one.
Then she looked
closely at my heart.
She wanted me
to start running.

A NOVEL ABOUT
AN AIRPORT

I'm writing a novel
about an airport
that falls in love
with one of the planes.
The blood is the people,
how they move from the plane
into the airport, from
the airport back into the plane.
The love's the blood.
The love's blood taking off.

A NOVEL ABOUT
A HEXAGON

I'm writing a novel
about a hexagon
that only has five sides.
It goes to school
for pentagons.
It feels so lonely,
pent up. Until another
hexagon shows up.
It's so beautiful.
It has five sides too.
They rub against each
other. They go on walks.
They start a very
successful business
together, a business
to end all businesses,
and just like that
theirs is the only business
which is the end of
business. In the end,
like always, it's a big
relief that comes.

TERRA INCOGNITA

You are on an airplane.
But then, suddenly,
you're in the middle
of the air, a red parachute
above you like a torn
flower. The plane looks
like a baby cow in the sky.
You have so many thoughts,
you can't really think of
a single one of them.
So you clear your mind.
You look out across
the horizon. There is
nothing special about
the horizon. It's just a line.
It's just a line when it
comes right down to it.
Below it is the sea.
Above it is the sky.
I'd like to throw
more dinner parties,
you think.

VERDANT LE VIDE

1.

The museum would not
accept the painting
unless there was some
figuration. A point,
a line, something.
He said, a point?
A line? Why not a bird?
A bird would be great,
agreed the museum.

2.

(a drawing of a bird)

SADDER THAN YOU

For my birthday party
I want to impress everyone
by standing at the bottom
of a giant vat while it fills
with concrete. The vat
is clear so everyone
can watch me disappear.
It's a kind of trick I play
on everyone I love.
But it's not a trick,
really. It's just the way
things happen.

MORNING

Everyone can see you.
You're fine. Everything
is just fine. Everything's
going to be ok.

GRANDMA'S BIRTHDAY

I'm having a good time
getting ready for my
grandma's birthday.
I'm writing on her cake.
She is in the corner.
She says nothing.
I try putting make
up on her face, but
that doesn't work.
She doesn't look well.
She doesn't look well
at all. I call the doctor.
The doctor delivers
the bad news:
the party's cancelled.

HERE KITTY

I'm on the roof training
the cat for the annual
Here Kitty agility contest.
It's an old roof. I shouldn't be
on it. There are warning
signs but I ignore them.
The cat is leaping back
and forth above one
particular hole. A few days later
I'm beneath a little
rubble unable to move,
and dehydrated. A spider's
crawling up my leg.
This must be it, I think.
This must be the end.
That's when you show
up with some water.
How's the cat? I ask.
It got last, you say.

LAST DAY

People are all in the room
getting the same info.
Things outside have
gotten so bad. Everyone
has a hand in the air,
waving like an upside
down flag, impatiently
waiting to ask a question.
The woman brings out
another arm.

A BUOY'S JOB IS TO BOB

No one's on the bus.
I drive it forever
straight as straight
can be on an endless
road at night.
But then it does end.
I go off a cliff
and into the sea.
Like my mother
said, I'll never
amount to anything.

AVIARY AREA

AVIARY AREA

In the beginning we're a bird.

In the beginning we are in every
   way a bird.

We are a diamond that pools
   into a bird.

So, a diamond pools into how
   we are a bird.

A diamond pools into any bird
   and we're a bird.

A stranger hands a stranger a glove
   and we're a bird.

We laugh, then we throw up
   a bird.

We hold our ribs, out comes
   a bird.

We learn beauty is a blue tuft
   of a bird.

We lean long in to the blue tuft
  of a bird

Beauty is two uneven blinks
  from a bird.

A blink then quickly a blink
  from a bird.

A kind sky of eyes hiding blinks
  of a bird.

A black word explodes from inside
  us, a bird.

A black word is also a bird.

So, we're a word and a black word
  is a bird.

So, we are the black word
  of a bird.

A blue beauty lifts up a black cloud
  like a bird.

We hear a petunia on a half-moon:
  a bird.

We hear what shrieks into specks:
    a bird.

What speck shrieks falls upon
    a falling bird.

We cannot drop what's not in
    our hands: a bird.

Our bird leg is a bright red
    burn of a bird.

To soothe our burn of a bird
    with a bird.

To owe what's owed over what's
    not a bird.

To write a blank blue check
    but on it's a bird.

What flaps like that in the ice
    machine's a bird.

What's frozen in our waves is a tip
    of a bird.

We fly on the tip of this ship
    in the sea, a bird.

What flies on the sea is also the sea
    and a bird.

What hides in the sky is a cloud
    plus a bird.

What is the sky but the blue blue
    pulse of a bird.

What hides in our cuts is the hair
    of a bird.

We are fat in the black triangles
    of a blue bird.

We land and take off in the hand
    of a bird.

We bend only inward toward the dark
    parts of a bird.

We try to buy the white eyes
    of a bird.

We can only buy the land left behind
    by a bird.

What sells claims its sick stake
    of a bird.

We call for calling sake the hotline
   of a bird.

We ask for a bird and the bird's all
   we are a bird.

We are a bird we are a bird is all
   we are a bird.

Who do you want we want us
   we're a bird.

We want us we want to speak
   to a bird.

To a bird we sound like nothing
   but a bird.

We hear nothing but the sleep
   of our bird.

If we dream of a bird as we sleep
   we're a bird.

We're a radish had deep in the salad
   of a bird.

We are a bird on the stranger finger
   of a bird.

We throw up we throw our hands
   up a bird.

We're a bird that presides over what's
   missing of a bird.

What we flip is the circuit breaker
   labeled bird.

What's what if what's love is a bird
   is a bird.

What's had in common is a lot
   of a bird.

We melt what's felt in the felt heart
   of a bird.

Take the face off of a bird and put it
   on a bird.

A cop is a bird but also a wolf
   is a bird.

What rises to weak applause
   is a bird.

What teeth's gleam in the bakery
   is a bird.

What is refuge but an unafforably
  ignorable bird.

Our bird is nothing but a sign of a bird.

Our bird is nothing but a sign of a bird
  of a future bird.

Our bird is all there is in the future
  of a bird.

Our bird phone calls from the closet
  of a bird.

Our bird hides idle in the sky.

Our bird rides its bike to Los Angeles.

Our bird is blue.

Our bird is white and knows why.

Our bird is red.

Our bird is pregnant until it isn't.

Our bird is two birds.

Our bird and a bird.

Our bird and a bird.

Our bird and a bird and a bird.

Our bird is a photo of a bird.

Our bird is of a photo of a lasagna.

Our bird is a vegetarian bird.

Our bird is on an airplane.

Our bird has a small hole.

Our bird is not like the others.

Our bird has a photo of a recipe.

Our bird licks the marmalade.

Our bird licks the top off the brook.

Our bird is ten years from making it.

Our bird is a photo of a bird in a cup.

Our bird gets on the bus.

Our bird understands the bus.

Our bird brings its groceries to the graveyard.

Our bird leans in like a tower.

Our bird is black.

Our bird does this.

Our bird goes here.

Shhh bird.

Our bird's new wing's in the front.

Our bird's sorrow comes in full pulses.

Our bird wears a ribbon on the wrong branch.

Our bird writes down the wrong mileage.

Our bird drinks the blood you know.

Our bird *shhh shhh.*

Shhh shhh bird.

Shhh bird.

Our bird is blue and red.

Shhh bird. *Shhh* bird.

Our bird hands us the philanges.

Our bird guts the merry carolers.
Shhh bird. *Shhh shhh.*

Shhh shhh bird. *Shhh shhh.*

Our bird is a gust of light.

Our bird is a wish of luck.

Our bird is a tinge of what's busted.

Our bird is a black cloud on the birds.

Shhh shhh. Shhh bird.

Our bird murdered a herd of birdbrains.

Our bird sailed a sea of wool.

Our bird is the pope's pope.

Our bird is Dutch and lusty.

Thank you thank you. Thank you bird.

Our bird is the problem: thank you bird.

Our bird pours egg cream in the punch bowl.

Our bird is on the devil's bad side.

Our bird is a species of beetle.

Our bird perches on a sunflower.

Our bird's grave is a bird.

Our bird tames the unrammable will.

Shhh bird.

Our bird walks into Burger Hut with a prediction.

Our bird predicts the wrong things correctly.

Our bird burns like every lamp in the night

Our bird knows no one.

Shhh shhh bird.

Our bird remembers nothing.
Shhh shhh bird.

Our bird sleeps in members only sleeves.

Our bird's burger's beefy.

Our bird is a moving comma.

Our bird's jowls snatch at the gelatin.

Our bird's emails are held in its belly.

Our bird's a starling.

Our bird is startling itself through a hoop.

Shhh bird.

Our bird's split while dreaming of apricots.

Our bird plucks apricots from the crests of waves.

Our bird is blue.

Our bird is blue.

Shhh bird. *Shhh shhh* bird.

Our bird freezes two chickens for the bonobo.

Our bird is a pan flattering the dead.

Our bird lingers in the stink of a new hour.

Our bird is stuck between the air and a night.

Our bird's fear turns the world solid.

Shhh shhh bird.

Shhh bird.

Our bird is an oak on the moon.

Our bird is footage of a futon.

Our bird fixes the springs for Death.

Our bird flies.

Our bird is the desire for a bonfire.

Our bird is an oracle of an evening
that won't come.

Our bird a bird call of light.

Our bird a bird call of night lights.

One bird a bird call of sighs.

Our bird puts it in the pit.

Our bird sleeps in the keyhole.

Shhh shhh. Shhh shhh bird.

Shhh shhh bird.

Our bird's beauty is tombier.

Our bird tunnels through the blackness.

Our bird tunnels through the blackness
 and into the black.

OARS

1.

Where are all our oars?
Here are all our oars
on the bottom of the sea
like more sea.

2.

People are all made of glass.
They can see through walls.
If there's not a law, there should be.
My only hope is that you have shoes.
It's an hour past the glass hour.
Stars are scraping against the sky.
Tiny triangles of glass
are in our blood.

3.

There's my uncle.
There's my aunt.
I look like them but I'm not.
I look made from the same ham.
The walls are on wheels.
The lights have a sugary cast.
I'm allergic to funnel-shaped foods.
My throat's a funnel.
I could die every midnight.
Cut my finger in the world.

4.

I don't know where I am.
Maybe on the ground in Australia.
Something's poison tongue licks my eyelash.
I stare back at it with one eye.
It grows even.
I touch a beating in a throat.
A nod hello?

5.

Being a non-tiger's not a good excuse.
Like a tiger, I could eat one.
On four, I go, but you don't.
Reliability is the best trait.
It beats talent.
Yeah, yeah, it really beats it.

6.

I have no chance to become mayor.
No one would vote for me.
I have all the wrong answers.
My pants have no pockets.
I don't know how to read.
I can't even hold a paper wad.
But I've never called an animal buttface.
I'm guilty only of speaking French to them.
The French echoes down a hall like a laugh.
It holds us like a flash flood forever.

7.

A person gets angrier as she gets closer.
I yell, Please go home.
There's no more water to dive into.
I long to be seen by the invisible.
Be unseen by the visible.
Be unseen by myself.
Never again, I yell.
Petunia of the half moon.
She shrieks into a speck.

8.

The maze is shaped like an 8.
I turn left so I'm more in the center.
It is not like a statue you can see.
I'm hungry, so naturally
I pick a fruit.
I put my feet up.
I'm ready for the omens.
Flowers and insects remind me of growing up.
Oh, yes, Mother's teacup.
The watermelon from the tragic picnic.
The rubber gloves for death.
The air is still.
The center never ceases to call.

9.

None of the lights are on.
I feel around for a fire exit.
I instead find a snake-bird.
I'm inside a circle of fire.
I move like how I see in theater.
A beautiful measurement for beauty.

10.

Some people die standing up.
They look like waves.
Flocks of birds from afar.
I move their hands around like 8's.
It is what you're supposed to do.
I recognize the jaunty one.
It looks like my friend.
My friend is a shape.
Like this everything piles up but me.

11.

I peek before the prayer's over.
There is nothing else to do.
There are no miracles.
Nothing is amazing.
The pieces of the mug my mother drank from hover.
One of the pieces looks like an arrowhead.
One like a crane trying to take off.

12.

I go numb so nothing hurts me.
I take up half the space.
I look down.
One of my legs starts above the knee.
No one notices.
Good thing I have three hands.

13.

A garden will save me money.
A bag looks like my dad and smells.
I don't remember the days of being good.
It isn't littering if the things are natural.
I only wish I had more to throw.

14.

The children get burns on their legs.
One blinks twice at me like a signal.
When I speak, everything falls apart.
The hand is a stranger's glove.
The danger feels soft, familiar.
I have a respiratory illness.
It is a bird in my throat.
It comes out.
It pools into a diamond.

15.

A tiger popped up.
It looked like he had a bird on his head.
It was really dark so who knows.
He couldn't see me very well either apparently.
He asked me if I was a kind of shark.

16.

I was waiting backstage at the *Tonight Show*.
There was a tiger.
I'm pretty good with tigers.
Then all the lights turned off.
I realized the show was over.
No one was around.
I found two beers in the refrigerator.
It was one of those small ones.

17.

I finally found my plans.
How will things ever be the same?
Our hearts are too hot.
That's one thing Vikings got wrong.

18.

It is now known as the missing pig.
It oinks into the sky over the valley.
It sounds like a mechanical baby.
In the light it looks like a wolf.
I clap for it even.
It touches the dark with its hoof.
The smaller one the harder one.

19.

I only drive a Toyota Corona.
I know what I'm doing.
I slow down.
I come to a stop.
I am underwater.
It's not like it is in the song.
My shoes are hand-me-downs.
I'm like a snowflake.
I'm like a bird in a cup.
I tap on the glass.
Erica? I think.
No, Helen?
It's a questionable method.
It's not that kind of bank.

20.

Her knees swell up like two cantaloupes.
The ice machine is gone.
From where is sympathy mustered.
Uh huh, uh huh, I understand.
It's right to offer the thirsty water.
A world without ice.
The carpet is red flames.
The table is birds.
The glass is like a vase.

21.

It's not just any river.
It's got that kind of blue glow.
It blinks twice.
It reminds me of my grandma's tail.
In that we all die horribly.
I'm bound to take the river toward the world.
I'm bound to tell the world my idea.
I'm bound to lose my idea to pain.
Stop it with heaven.

22.

I've never felt so in shape.
I feel like a skyscraper with a big band playing on top.
My arches arch high.
Some of my parts hit huge children.
The world can surprise you only with its kindness.

23.

It feels good outside of the burning car.
Things look newly like a taco.
Even the flowers bloom.

24.

I haven't talked to my sisters in years.
Will you receive our headshots, they ask.
I receive their headshots with trepidation.
I've never received this many headshots.
I deliver the headshots to the administration building.
There's a hole in the sky on the administration building.
No, that's a crow.
There's a whole murder up there.

25.

It sounded like you said attaching a self to the wall.
It looks crooked.
My neighbor walks in with my t-shirt on.
He tells me about re-math.
But I already know all about re-math.
He gives me a problem.
Ten, I say.
We all nod our heads until our necks ache.
I suddenly remember my winter coat.
I wonder where my winter coat is.
There's dust everywhere.
It's like dunes in the desert.
It really did sound like you were saying self.
Like, the self falls.
Like, nailing in the self.

26.

I'm on a new highway.
It goes forever if I want.
Then I pull off of it.
I order the first thing on the menu.
Is it Christmas?
I think that in another language.
But which one?
I'm not ready.
So, I just order the box.
I'll just have the box.
I say it like boxxxx.
It's a good thing I had five dimes.
Is it Christmas?
"What?" says the woman.
Is it Christmas?
It feels like I'm in an on microwave.
It feels like day two of endless war.

27.

I look all over for my friend.
I get lost looking for him.
I put a microphone to the ghost's mouth.
That dick clams up.

28.

I name the boat George Washington.
It slaps on the gentle waves.
I ride George Washington to the art museum.
Wait, this isn't the art museum.
I didn't know I knew how to play guitar.
My fingers just go.
I move them around like a dying spider on the stairs.
Out comes "Sharp Dressed Man."
These riffs make thee weep.
People might as well be flowers.
These flowers too make thee weep.
Look how they falter and bend.
One's hemline is a lived life.
One can tuck a cuff.

29.

It's like rising joy was lit from its own flame.
Our faces went back to normal.
I called for the full blow.
The ratios were in my favor.
Now would be a good time to be huge.
Everybody turned around.
Some got into their cars.
I didn't remember where I parked.
Then I did remember.
I remembered everything just as it once was.
This poem is for my dog, Gracie.

30.

Pasta is my favorite food.
It's time to eat!
I make a face with the noodles.
It looks familiar.
The plate bites my fingers off.
I drop the plate and it breaks.
That's enough pasta.

31.

I rub the ball and say it's a boy.
My co-workers stay duped forever.
We wish we could've met him, they say.
I've only heard of the rock of Gibraltar.

32.

It's like a sea of heat.
The kid shows up with shorts on.
Where'd you get those shorts, The Gap?
Do you have any change?
(Kids always have big bills.)
This kid had exact change.
He's a champ at math.
He sews his own clothes.
In this world so few sew.
So so few do.

33.

I'm a buffalo, which is great.
Sadly, though, I'm the last buffalo.
But, luckily, I know how to read.

34.

I look at the mountains for crying.
They're so shiny and clean.
Words are flowing down into the valley.
They're in the order of Clan of the Cave Bear.

35.

There are like 5 pho shops in the area.
I'm in the first minute of being hungry.
I look at my hair.
I look at the noodles.
I laugh but also throw up.
A bird looks like it's falling asleep.
My to-do list is all checked.
So I go mow Cher's hair.

36.

I work so hard, but for what?
I don't care to really know anything anymore.
I've never seen a new mountain.
Fake cobras outnumber the real ones.
The fakeness has overtaken us.
The sea, you see is the key to a good life.
It laps forth, like gears.
It laps forth, like crepe.
It laps. It laps, cellophanic.

37.

No one knows what BOGO means.
I'd lick my own forehead off if I could.
Anyway, things don't work out for me.
I hid the cash in the wrong cave.
I'm the only thing tigers eat.
My head's above the light.
I squint my eyes only to see fighters.

38.

I'll only drive a Toyota Corona.
Anything will go forever if you love it.
Like a heart.
Like a wire cloud.
I wasn't born.
I shook from a sine wave or curve.
I dip into the ripples.
Like a mother, I will never die.
Like a heart.
Like a wire cloud.

39.

I'm on an island or back in time.
The sea is there.
Like needles coming through from beneath.
I'm prey.
I'm prey.
I don't take the bait.
One death comes like steps.
One comes like a bird on a leg.
One fades like specks in the black.
I wave my hand in front of my eyes.
The sea is here.

40.

I read a book on sex to you on a dune.
One, let go into being led: two insects.
A big sun goes down on us.
I leave just so I can see you.
A hallway easily leads to a door to a zoo.
What zoo's left.
What's left to believe in one tiger.

41.

I'd never heard of Kentucky.
I thought it was a kind of beef.
Days later I'm deep inside it.
I'm face to face with an elf.
The elf's mouth won't move unless I lick it.
I lick a whole life from it.
A strawberry softening in the sun.

42.

Never take a class on how to fly.
They just tell you to stand on one leg.
I jump and on the way up I know.
Two birds fly around my head: a crown of laughter.
My body is/is not a thing.
Like eyes of bees.

43.

A kindness casts a shadow.
It takes a knee to die.
You might be sick with some sadness.
We're all sick with some sadness.
We weep at the end of everything.
Endless applause even.
Clapping like a broken gate.
If your heart was a gate
I'd break it.

44.

One thing we do is stare at seas.
We see what washes up.
Just bars of soap.
We go home, wash up.
There is a joke deep inside the world.
There's an unbendable silence.
Like how you look to a tarantula.

45.

My blue jeans are so big.
No one can wear them.
Some jerk is talking about it.
He says *numinous* and *esoteric*.
But what do those words mean.
They're magic words.
They make you bigger.
Look at you what you're becoming.
Right, the opposite of a planet.

46.

Sorry about my overflowing trash.
I'm the leader of a new cult.
It's just that we only eat packaged foods.
We go to the zoo.
We talk to the zebra.
We yell watch out for the blue cloud.
Watch out for the foamy waterfall.
Watch out for the flashing volcano.
I will write you a letter sometime.
Any letter.

47.

I get a letter back.
It's from me at five.
Mom's eating my cake
I've left in the dark.

48.

From this bush, I call my name.
There's no one here with my name.
I have no faith in the future.
Everything is mapped.
A ghost on the long couch.
Fuckers take heart.

49.

We are in a cave.
We know because of the drips.
How the light lights the dark up.
Now is a time to take a photo.
You are licking a cone.
You look good licking the cone.
You end in the middle.
The end is nigh.
But what ends is wee.

50.

We're at the end.
At the end is where I save myself.
Nothing's left to whizz in arcs.
Everyone else has been eaten by night's mouth.
Night's quiet on my face.
On my back on the bank.
Of the sea of the world.
On the black on the sky.
Til I see all our oars
on the bottom of the sea
like more sea.

HAIRCUTS

1.

Dad used to take me to Sam
his barber. It was a shop
called Sam's. Sam was
always in there by himself
reading the newspaper
waiting for Dad. This was
before you were born.
We liked to talk about how
much things used to cost.
The candy in the machine
took one quarter and it
came out too fast. A haircut
is the first sacrifice—
a handing over of proof of
next to nothing. Take it
and I'll be brave with ease.
My favorite part was Dad's
turn in the chair. I watched
him become new again,
closer to me.

2.

We sometimes cry during
the first haircut. Maybe it's
the scissors. Or maybe it's
not knowing why we're
being asked to give up
this part of ourselves
that's the most alive.
Your hair was so white
it was barely there—
a tiny white fog
and then it wasn't there
but then it was curly.
Years later, we got little plants
for everyone for Christmas
because we were broke.
They're all dead now—
the plants, I mean.
Except Grandma's.
I saw it still on her sill
in that photo you sent
to me on the phone.
It's like a race that doesn't
end when we win.

3.

I used to talk to dad
as he stretched his legs
forever in the living room
before jogging. It seemed
like he could stretch
all day long. If you do
the math, maybe whole
years were spent just
stretching, pivoting
his upper body slowly
across the plane of his legs.
The three of us were
so ready to love you.
I couldn't sleep at night
imagining you. I thought
you'd look exactly like me,
like another me, same face,
same arms, same hair,
riding in my backpack.
But when you arrived—
my last day of 7th grade,
you were a girl.
You had nothing
like the moon
for hair.

4.

In a diner in Florida,
you had no hair
under your ball cap.
The server flipped
the bill of it and asked
what the little guy
wanted. You pulled
your cap down even
further. Can it matter
what's really wanted
in a swamp? What does
the little guy want?
She'll have the pancake,
Mom finally said.

5.

L cut my hair once on
a hot balcony in Kaohsiung.
We were far above everything.
The sun was finally sinking
down into Monkey Mountain.
It was your 24th birthday.
I hadn't gotten you anything.
I tried to call but the times
were off. I'm sure you were
just waking up in Omaha,
somewhere near where
we were both born. B asked
L to cut his whole beard off.
He looked like a baby in
a man's body. His face was
a kind of blue fruit I had
never seen before. Where
was I? Where was I going?
This new family. B like
a brother with a strange
new mouth. L, a sister
with my dead hair on her
sticky neck. After they
went back inside, I swept
some of our hair off the
balcony, into the unbreathable

air over all the heads of
all the people, over
the sleeping market
with the decapitated
pig hanging next to
its own head. My hair
went up and never
came down.

6.

There is a photo
I took of you laughing.
We were on the back
patio in Kimberling
City. It is a good photo.
I took it with the nice
camera Mom bought me.
In it, you have no hair.
You're doubled over,
overwhelmed with
what's funny. Forgive
me. It's a slice of time
so tiny you can't even
look at it.

7.

A haircut is a lot
to ask of anyone.
I can see that now.
L also cut mine
once in the desert
because I asked
and I felt broken—
because I asked
and was broke.
B waited his turn
across from me
with a can of beer.
It wasn't the haircut
I wanted—it was
to have it cut, to
be cared for, or
thought of, to
sit still when
asked to, to
live through
the entirety of
something.

8.

Grandma is always
worrying about her
hair. How's my hair,
she asks in hospice.
It's been the same
since 1970. She used
to seal it in Aquanet.
It's never gone
anywhere.

9.

That terrifying year
was my second year
of college. K showed
me Pavement's "Cut
Your Hair." I tried to show
you that song, but
you didn't get it.
My hair is getting
thin in the front.
I'll probably cut it
all off, like how
Dad's is now.
B thinks it will
look good like that.
I want to move
closer. I want to
get chickens
or a dog.

10.

Dad's barber, Sam,
died about 20 years ago.
Now Dad shaves his
own head with clippers
he bought from Sam's
Club.

11.

The second time
your hair fell out
you were ready.
We spent so much
time watching swimmers
on television. None
of them had hair
either. That summer,
when you got on
the blocks, no
swim cap on,
everyone knew
how real
you were.

12.

I was never prepared
to lose you. I lived
far away—a safe
distance from the sound
of battle. Some nights
I couldn't sleep
imagining you not
at home. Though
some nights I could
sleep. I wonder
how you slept,
your skull smooth
on the pillow.
B tells me stories
about her sister
who is trapped
in time at 9.
How heavy can
surrendered love
feel in our throats.
How easy it is
to text you a joke,
to swap photos
on our phones.
Today you turn 27.
I will cut my hair—

the smallest gesture
and think of you.
I will think of how
it felt to put my
whole hand on
your bald head.
How I can never
be prepared for
anything like that.

THE FUTURE / THE BABY

THE FUTURE

You wake up in a pool of blood.
The knife is on the stairs.
The telephone is ringing.
It's the scientist.

THE FUTURE

A feeling of feeling
right feeling wrong.
You're a girl
or boy, holding
a leash with
a cow or bird
running or
flying away
from it
nearby or far
away.

THE FUTURE

There's only one
pattern, and everyone
makes that one
behind someone.
We're all going
to be somebody.
We're all going
places. We're all
placing our
selves in
meatier
positions.
What dies
in our
hands are
flowers.
You're a mother
forever.

THE FUTURE

After years of
being gone
she came back.
She was different.
She was a different
person. We had
a neat breakfast.

THE FUTURE

The sun is
so beautiful
when it's going
away and down,
but it's not
really doing either
and the sea
is so see-through.
On the side
of the sea
yr dad is
saving me
with his pants
on.

THE FUTURE

A hundred happy
families dying
together on a tram.
There was once
a beginning.
You are so small.
You are so so
small. You sew.
You move boxes.
You plug things in.

THE FUTURE

I'll be the murderer
of my own murderer
and the murderer
of the murderer
of my own murderer.

THE FUTURE

I look all over
for you in your
childhood but
when I find you
I have nothing
to say. I make you
a sandwich to
take up some
time, to think
of what to tell you.
You aren't hungry.
I say I have something
I'm about to say.

THE BABY

A foot steps out
of the rectangle
into the circle.
A baby's on
the carpet.
Your face is
just five different-
sized circles.

THE BABY

It takes a long time
for the baby to
come out. Then it's
not strong enough.
It can't be ridden
great distances.
It takes it a long time
to become an adult.
Look, look how it doesn't
know where anything is.

THE FUTURE

Once everyone arrives
I go ahead with the plan.
I get naked all the way.
I turn on the T.V.
Look at me on T.V.
I dance around on T.V.
I dance-walk to a small
park, and climb a tree.
People gather around.
I'm the naked man
from T.V. Before
I make my speech
I take questions.
Everyone wants water.

THE FUTURE

I'm standing in a field.
There are trophies
everywhere like
poppies. They're
for participation.
Everything is an award
for nothing.

THE SEA

The sea is.

THE FUTURE

I find a boat with a man in it.
It's in the Shang Dynasty.
It's going into battle
with some clan
but I have a lot of luggage.
The man helps me load
some of my luggage.
I feel like my luggage
is taking up too much space.
It's ok, he assures me.
There's plenty of room,
he says, but really
there isn't. The boat is
so slow and heavy,
it begins to sink.
I'm sorry, says the man.
He holds me while
we float on top of
my last remaining piece
of luggage, little red iceberg.
I've never fallen in love.
He's so kind.
All he ever wanted
was to go to war.

THE FUTURE

It looks like we
aren't going to make it.
You burned the bed.
You just set it on fire
one morning while
I was still in it.
Days later, we watched
the garbageman
look at it. He
hung like a hummingbird
over the smell.
All that power
he alone had and
never knew that
for a moment he
alone wielded it.

THE BABY

We're in the kitchen
fighting over
which of us will
keep the baby.
I'm going to leave
the house and I'm
never going to come
back, you say.
I'm holding the baby.
You say it's yours
and I say it's mine.
You reach for its little arm.
I pull it back until it cries.
You want it so bad.
There is a darkness,
and a buoy in the darkness.

THE FUTURE

The scientist folded
a paper airplane.
She wrote my name
on the side, but
it was spelled wrong.
Some scientist, I thought.
But then I thought
maybe I said it aloud.
I convinced myself that
I only thought it.
But a great scientist
could have invented
a way to hear
my thoughts aloud.
What an incredible scientist,
I thought. What a
good person I am.
What a beautiful person
What a beautiful sun.

THE BABY

The missing baby
had been missing
his whole life, since
birth, but still,
everyone grieved
and everyone looked
everywhere for him.
They looked in the trees
and the basements.
They drained the ponds.
They let the hounds
run wild. After a while,
some people thought
the missing baby's family
killed him, but
the missing baby
never had a family.
Some people thought
he was killed by coyotes.
Some people thought
he fell in love and
just moved away.
But none of this was true.
The missing baby
was simply missing.
and always had been.

THE FUTURE

I'm in a carousel.
The kind that spins
people to the wall.
There is a woman
and a man and a man
inside of it too,
and a man operating it.
Everybody I love is
looking down at me,
laughing. When I die,
I'll die alone.
I know that much,
held down by my
own shadow, wanting
to touch the woman,
the man, the man,
across the curvature.
I won't be able to even
look. I'm on a train.
I'm a tiny spider.
A tiny star.
Or a giant spider.
When everything stops,
I'll open the only door
to the carousel and
it'll be the wrong one
I've forgotten entering.

THE FUTURE

In the desert, I'm wearing
an appropriate hat.
There's a long line
of people behind me
not wearing hats.
The first person
in line asks me where's
everyone's going?
I don't know. So I just say
I'm going into the middle
of the dark. Where are
you going? I ask. We were
following you, she says.
Then you are going
into the middle of the dark,
I say. She doesn't want to go
into the middle of the dark.
She's a holding a baby.
She tells the second person
in line where we're going,
into the middle of the dark,
but the second person
doesn't want to go into
the middle of the dark either.
The second person tells
the third person, who

also doesn't want to go
into the middle of the dark.
No one wants to go into
the middle of the dark.
But I'm going into
the middle of the dark,
I say. It was just as true
as ever. Where I'm going
it is dark. And I'll be
right in the middle of it.

THE BABY

I'm a baby.
I'm playing with
a toy boat
in the dirt.
I'm bleeding into
my cowboy hat.
It fills all the
way up. It makes
a little pool.
It's not my hat.
I don't know where
the hat came from.
I put the toy boat
in the pool in the hat.
My mother looks for me.
I can hear the sound.
The woods go forever.

THE FUTURE

I'm in the desert
at a backyard party.
A pack of coyotes
are tearing apart
a herd of cats
on the other side
of the wall. It
sounds like children
laughing. The person
I'm talking to says
it's coyotes killing cats.
It's such an awful sound,
says the person.
Then the person
drinks his wine.
We can do so much
damage, so quickly,
with just our hands,
I think. I look at
my hands while
the cats rip. They
look like everyone else's
hands. They can do
such awful things.
I just have to tell them
what to do, and they'll

do it. How is your wine?
I ask. It's good,
says the person.
How's your wine?
asks the person.
Mine's good too.

THE FUTURE

I am trapped inside
a room of people
speaking a language
that sounds like
a baby machine.
I only want to be
with you. I send you
money and a note.
Take this money,
I begin to write.
Someday, let's go to
Ophal together.
Please buy the tickets.
Please wait for me
there. Wait for me
in this place
I made up.

THE BABY

There is a seat
next to you
in the dark balcony
of a movie theater
so I sit in it.
I've been waiting
for you, you say.
A scary movie called
The Baby starts.
The baby is levitating
above a pond.
You lick your hand
then put it in my pants.
You lick my hand
then put it in your pants.
The baby is killing
its parents with an ax
hiding their heads
in a toy box.

THE FUTURE

I'm on a small
white boat with
three wounded chickens.
They're finally quiet.
The world is so quiet.
I think maybe the
chickens died, but
then they start squawking
and shaking again.
One of them is missing
a wing and the back
half of her body.
Another looks inside
out, its head just hanging
there, its eyes blinking.
I try to kill them with
an ax, but I cut the boat
in half. I cut my legs
in half too. I cut my head
in half too. With half
a head, I cut my body
in half. I cut the sea,
I cut the mountains,
I cut the sky, the clouds,
the airplanes, and all
the people in the airplanes

all in half. I can't stop.
I feel like a god there
in that boat with my ax
so I cut the world in half.
Then I get adopted
by a family that lives
on a farm. One day
my new father asks me
to kill the chickens
for dinner. He puts an ax
in my one hand. I do not
remember half of everything.

THE FUTURE

We are in a graveyard.
Everyone I love
is dead, you say. What
about me? I say.
You're not dead, you say.
I mean, do you love me?
I say. I only love
the dead, you say. But
you're not dead either,
I say. I'm dead when
no one's around to love
me, you say. We stand
in front of a dead tree.
Do you love this tree?
I say. No, you say.
But it is dead, I say.
You don't seem to know
what being alive means,
you say.

THE BABY

The refrigerator is open.
There is a baby in a jar.
It's time for breakfast.
The universe is still expanding.
Yr hands are moving like
you're wrangling a snake.
Will you do a magic trick?
someone asks. I start
to do the magic trick.
I get on a plane to Costa Rica.
They serve me cake
but it is not cake.
It is two babies.
I try to tell them what
cake is. No one on the plane
to Costa Rica knows what
cake actually is. I don't
want to ever eat again.
The babies are crying.
I am dying in a pool of blood.

THE FUTURE

There are these two coyotes
on the path in front of me.
They don't budge as I
come speeding toward them
on my bicycle and kind of go
hey hey hey. I imagine them
leaping on me as I pass,
maybe biting at my ankles
while I try to push through.
One coyote on each ankle,
dragging them both along.
But that doesn't happen.
I go right past them
and they don't even move,
and they don't attack.
They just watch me ride by.
One of them licks a paw
like maybe it is hurt
or like maybe it is hungry.
I don't look back.
I just want to get to all that light,
the pink light at the end
of some dark tunnel
like a still pool in all
the brightly-lit familiarness.

THE FUTURE

I yell crater into the crater.
I couldn't think of anything
else to yell into it. Things
need to know from other things
what they really are,
I think. Then I yell empty
space. That's more accurate
I think. Then I feel a real
responsibility land on my
shoulders. I like it there,
how the weight feels there.
I yell space created by an
outside force. Then I just
yell space again. Then
I just yell a general yell
for as long as I can.
I yell you and then I yell me,
as if I'm yelling us into existence,
into what we already are,
or were, or will be.
And then I yell space,
space, space into a chicken
coop. Space, space, space.
Until finally the chicken
coop is empty, and finally
it is quiet.

THE BABY

You are a baby
swooped up by a giant
bird and dropped
dozens of years later onto
a nun on a horse
in a boat on the sea.
This is the kind of
death that holds you,
a slow death you ride
into forever
like an asteroid.
It's the death
you die waiting for.
The nun's name
is Beehive. The horse
is Forehead.

THE HORSE FELL INTO THE SEA

1.

You woke up. A bell rung.
You followed what rung
through the window. The moon.
A cliff overlooking the sea.
A nun. On a horse.
In a boat. You yelled to warn
it. The horse. But what
about? Then you clapped.
That startled the horse.
The nun fell. Off the horse.
Into the boat. The horse
fell. Into the sea.

2.

up up a bell a bell up   a lullaby a bell
up up a bell a bell   up a lullaby hello

moon in the window   moving like this this
bell in the window   moving like this this

walk back from sleep   walking back past
walk back sleep walk   back past back past

a side of the sea   been never been
a side of the town   down been down

the bend looking   down off the cliff
bend down looking   off the black cliff

I was like *oh ok*   eyes like oar
eyes like oar over oar   or over oar

was like *oh yeah*
eyes like this yeah

was like *ok ok*
eyes like this ok

was like *yes ok   ok*
eyes light our oar

nun on nun on
all on horse on

nun on horse on
on horse a nun

a moon not *the* moon
was like *oh oh ok*

so eyes like our oar
eyes light our oar

eyes like oak oars
like this oak oar

eyes like light light
eyes light the oar

nun on nun on
horse on boat

boat in the sea
a nun on nun on

or me in the sea
what's in the sea

a moon not *the* moon
a moon or *ooo* a moon

a boat on boat on
who's that in a boat

me not *the* me below me
a nun or moon

a moon not *the* moon
a nun not *the* nun

was like *oh it's six*
like how is it six

it's six from my eyes
eyes above our oar

what's rung on a boat
what's that on a boat

a boat and a bell
a bell and a bell

a bell deep below me
under a nun or moon

me booing a moon
me or me below me

a.m. a.m. a.m. a.m.
me booing the moon

eyes lighting the oar
am booing am booing

eyes like oar light
horse in the light

oar eyes oar eyes
oar eyes the light

horse comes in the light
horse under the moon

was like *oh yeah*
under the nun like *oh yeah*

eyes in a boat's eyes
eyes above boat eyes

boat's eyes our oar
our oar are our oar

eyes nays in the sea
eyes nays eyes nays

nays nays in the sea
on a boat in the sea

horse eyes light oars
eyes like oar oar

oar a horse in the sea
horse eyes in the sea

eyes nays in a boat
was like *oh yeah*

trapped in the sea
trapped in the sea

clapped on the cliff
making black black

horse and a bell
oar a horse an oar

trapped in the sea
was like *oh yeah*

a moon not a moon
one wave amounting

yes eyes in the sea
sea eyes sea eyes sea

easy easy our eyes
get sick in the sea

clap black black black
black black each clap

black in the light
back down in the light

on top of the sea
eyes clap the black

or a bell in the sea
horse eyes in the sea

sea eyes sea eyes
eyes sea eyes sea

black waves a wave
eyes a wave a wave

one wave amounting
horse went amounting

into into a mount
into into a mount

down down went down
went down down

went horse when oar
broke like bells

broken over the sea
broken into the sea

like bells broken oar
like broken horse

drown drowning horse
drown downing down

a moon not *the* moon
to the bottom with bells

nun in the boat
nun in the boat

nays in the sea
nays stay in the sea

nays nays says nays
nays nays says nays

says nays says nays
nays down in the sea

drown on our own
drown drown drown all

with broken bells or bells
horses into the black

me on the cliff like *ok*
walk back around

nun like *oh ok*
ghost down the bend

inside the side of town
eyes for hours hours

down in the side of town
eyes like what's ours

eyes into the black
what did I watch

a love like drowning
drown drowning down

what did I watch
but what did I see

horse drowning down
drowning down in the sea

ha ha was like *oh no*
like *oh no no* our oar

a horse not a nun
oh no no what's ours

what goes amounting   but a wave but a wave
what goes amounting   but a wave in the sea

six hours for horse   what's hours is ours
ours and ours and ours   our hours for hours

a voice like *it was me*   ghost now in the sea
eyes nays eyes nays   eyes says nays nays

was like *oh no ok*   or our hours are eyes
like *oh so ok ok*   or what's ours are eyes

more nays in the black   more eyes nays in the black
what nays in the black   was nays in the black

what's drowned now nays   now nays now nays
what's down just nays   now a days in the black

turn back to the nays
run run run to the days

to the light in the sun
white light in the sun

on a horse in the sun
a horse not *the* horse

or our oar are eyes
eyes light up like a oar

a cliff in the sun and a sea
like *oh ok* what cliffff

now fall off the cliff off
fall off the cliff off

run run to the sun
inland to the sun

a sun not *the* sun
the sssssssssssssun

eyes like our oar
eyes light like ours

oh no oh no ha ha
no no no no oh no

like what cliffffffff
like what what cliff

the cliffff to the sea
the cliffff into the sea

into the sun clappping
that's me in the air

arms of horse clapping
like what's that and that

what that's and that
that and that that

that and what's that
what's that in the sea

one wave amounting
a wave is waves

in the sea in the sea
in the sssssssssea

what that's and that
that and what's that

comes *oh ok* in waves
comes ok in the waves

a buoy in the sea
a buoy booing at a moon

a bbbuoy in the sea
bobbing in the sea

buoy in what nays
buoy in the darknesss

buoy buoy in the sea
buoy buoy in the sea

bells for your ghosts   bells for your ghosts
hooves are bells   bells for your ghosts

bobbing like a coffin   in the black of the sea
bobbing like a coffin   in that part of the sea

THE LAST LEG

//

A mountain's job's to jut,
a buoy's job's to bob.

//

You choose the slow
boat. You're pretty
scared. There's a guy
named Peter or Peter
II. He's the first
to be decapitated.

//

On your death
bed I spill
juice. You know
now you're alive,
because the creak.
Remember that
teen on a cord
in a bean field.

//

Look at a balloon
I put over
the perfect
turgid horses.

//

I want her you
are not her
problems are
lifelong.

//

There's nothing
abnormal about me
being a normal lake.

//

I stood on the beach
watching the kids bob.
I can't help but think
I got your wish wrong.

//

A bouquet of
flowers stuck
in the laundry
chute.

//

They're acting
like it matters.
One got a ticket
to Costa Rica.
No one knows
where nothing is.
No one knows
nothing's there.

//

You take the arm
to Cinemagic.
Where we're headed
can't be right.
If I could be anyone
I would.

//

You always tell
this story about
how a bird took
a poop into yr mouth
while you were
on your back in bed.
But what about
the roof, liar.

//

One joke is I hide
when no one
is looking
for me and
I just come out.

//

I go beneath
the bed.
You are so sad
without me
you're a blue paper
swan.

//

The third time
you lay with
the mime.
Is that you
you think
it whispers.

//

We shouldn't do
this. A fly.
More flies.
You're two times
more whole
after the split.

//

So far north
it's French.
Her and me
and you and
me and you
all facing her
and you.

//

The enemy wears
yr uniform. I eat
a yellow orange.
Real life is
the easiest kind
to fake.

//

The cat fell
asleep on
top of me.
When I woke up
it was dead.
(True story.)

//

In the shadow,
someone takes off
a shirt, lights
a cigarette. They
caught the wrong
man, I thought.
But it might've just
been the wrong
shadow.

//

Someone just threw
a donut at my head.
I mean, just now.
Right now. I'm
really somebody.
I'm going to go vote
for myself.

//

The trophy delivery
arrived, finally.
Her body kind of
leaned over
to make the transfer.
I build a house.
It shines so bright
no one sees
(the sun).

//

Chances are
someone who's
dead baked a
cake for you
but not for me.

//

There's only one
thing and it's
just sliced up.
I like to listen to birds
but also to waves.

//

How you fall in the woods
always with a candelabra.

//

Every time I'm left
I'm left for dead.

//

You're not quite
yourself. You're
more like this
or that. You're
more like this.
You look really
close to the lamp.

//

I can draw a straight line.
A boy of nine
in red near
no mountains.

//

Now you'll
need
a mirror
to take
the massacre
off.

//

The Who'ves is
a group I'm in.
We come in
on top of horses.
Everyone not us claps.
If they don't,
there's trouble,
and we eat.

//

There is no
such thing
as infinity.
I started counting
when I was
very young.
Now I'm done.

ACKNOWLEDGEMENTS

Academy of American Poets
Arkansas International
Bennington Review
Birdfeast
Black Warrior Review
Columbia Poetry Review
Fence
Fugue
Houseguest
Hunger Mountain
Hypothetical
Interrupture
jubilat
The Iowa Review
PEN America
poets.org
Portland Monthly
Redivider
Submission

OTHER BOOKS BY ZS

NOVELS

Mammother (Featherproof 2017)

POETRY

The Book of Joshua (Black Ocean 2014)

Fjords, vol 1 (Black Ocean 2012)

Scary, No Scary (Black Ocean 2009)

The Man Suit (Black Ocean 2007)

NOTES

Inside We Make Children Sandwiches are stories written for children.

Aviary Area was written for Mathias Svalina. The title is his.

Much of *Now is a Good Time* is written with reference to, and under the influence of, the poems of James Tate. The titles, "Sanjoo Hoo" and "The Distance of Loved Ones" are his.

"The Snowy Plover of Reno" was written for Jeff Alessandrelli.

Forty-three of the poems in "Oars" were originally published under the title *Hear Oars* by Two Plum Press (Portland, OR) in 2017. That chapbook is available at twoplumpress.com.

Haircuts was written for my sister, Kelsey Peters (née Schomburg). It was self-published in 2016. It was performed in its entirety at Poetry Press Week at Disjecta in Portland, OR in 2016 by Derek Wilson (violin), Vikesh Kapoor (voice), and Fergus Kinnell whose hair was shaved completely during the performance.

The Future / *The Baby* was written for Brandi Katherine Herrera.

"The Future" (pg. 164) is written under the influence of Raymond Carver's short story, "Popular Mechanics."

THANK YOU

To my sister, Kelsey, who lent me money for the laptop I used to write all of these poems. To Mathias Svalina, from whose soil my poems sprout. To my parents, Bruce and Nancy.

To my community poetry workshop students who helped support me while I wrote. To Dennis Schmickle, whose cover designs are now the beautiful faces of my poems. To Janaka Stucky, who in my poems believes and invests. To everyone at Black Ocean, for your time, and for a catalog for this book to live within. To everyone else who inspired me, and who supported me, so I could write these poems, especially Joseph Mains, JMW, Kate Bingaman-Burt, Sara Guest, Jacques Rebotier, Hajara Quinn, Brandon Shimoda, Lisa Schumaier, John Beer, Wong May, Mary Ruefle, Heather Christle, James Tate, and Dara Wier.

And to my partner, Brandi Katherine Herrera, especially, who puts the color in the world for me to see.